Introduction to Online Payments Risk Management

T0324037

Ohad Samet

O'REILLY®

Beijing · Cambridge · Farnham · Köln · Sebastopol · Tokyo

Introduction to Online Payments Risk Management

by Ohad Samet

Printed in the United States of America.

Published by O'Reilly Media, Inc., 1005 Gravenstein Highway North, Sebastopol, CA 95472.

O'Reilly books may be purchased for educational, business, or sales promotional use. Online editions are also available for most titles (*http://my.safaribooksonline.com*). For more information, contact our corporate/institutional sales department: 800-998-9938 or *corporate@oreilly.com*.

Editors: Mike Loukides and Meghan Blanchette

June 2013: First Edition

Revision History for the First Edition:

2013-06-06: First release

See *http://oreilly.com/catalog/errata.csp?isbn=9781449365400* for release details.

ISBN: 978-1-449-36540-0

[LSI]

Table of Contents

Part III.   Tools and Methods

Preface

Why Was This Book Written, and Who Is It For?

Losses and fraud are as old as human society. Scams and acts of fraud were not started nor invented by the digital generation. The most widely known scam, the "Nigerian Prince" or "Advance Fee" scam, luring victims to pay large sums in exchange for a big and never-arriving payout, is not a digital invention. It is a modern variant of the "Spanish Prisoner" scam, which originated in the 19th century. In any situation involving the opportunity for gain, be it a game for chips or an actual money transfer, some people are going to try to bend the rules. They do so even when there is no way to cash out, in order to get ahead and maintain status if nothing else. Almost everyone cheats; some of us are professionals.

As more and more financial activity goes online, the potential payout becomes larger. It was once only possible to steal a credit card. Now you can lend money, refinance your loan, or start a new business online. Increasingly, consumers go shopping online. 2012's Cyber Monday saw sales of almost $1.5 billion, the biggest in history. Consumers have their lives online on Facebook and Twitter. Identities are easy to steal, replicate, and invent; Facebook reports that about 9% of its profiles are fake. On top of all that, consumer activity creates enormous amounts of data that require novel techniques for simple searches, let alone understanding who's real and who isn't, who's a fraudster and who's telling the truth. When operating a financial services business you are faced not only with fraud, but with other causes for losses driven by multiple factors: credit default, misunderstandings, bad operational procedures, and more. I realized that there needs to be a single source for a methodical and comprehensive way to find, describe, understand, and deal with these problems so that businesses could succeed online.

This book aims to be that source—to give an introduction, overview, and overarching framework for dealing with risk in online payments. The material in it has been accumulated, shaped, tested, and proven to work over several very busy years of working in various payments companies, specifically in risk management and fraud prevention for payments, as well as consulting and discussing with many others. It aims to spark a discussion around the practice of risk management in payments in particular and eCommerce in general, as well as give the layout of what one should think about when approaching this vast field. It brings together data, organization, technology, UX, product, and other insights to present a blueprint for the best-possible loss and risk management organization in a rapidly changing digital environment, from a one-person task force to dozens of agents and analysts. It covers the essentials of the first couple of years and points toward following steps.

This book isn't a complete step-by-step manual, as that would require thousands of pages; it is an introduction with some needed elaborations. It also skips a lot of basic knowledge that can be obtained through other sources and, therefore, isn't always a 101-level book, although I made sure to explain every term that may be less than obvious. There is no deep discussion of machine learning, model building, frequentist vs. Bayesian statistics, or preferred packages for visualization; these topics are covered at a reasonable to extensive level in many other books, and their detailed and specific application is only required after the tools in this book have been exhausted. Neither does this book include typical application review procedures or price ranges for common data sources; the first is too specific to your system and data availability, and the second is available online using simple searches. But it will get you started and take you far along your way. More than anyone, this book is aimed at those who are tasked with starting a RMP function, whether in a small or large corporation. Veterans will find best practices that they have worked with through the years and new ideas that they may want to adopt. CFOs, COOs, and CEOs that have a RMP team reporting to them will learn more about its internals and what to expect of it, as well as some insight into how to measure its performance.

Acknowledgements

I have many people to thank for the incredible experiences I've had through my career—first and foremost my teams. Over the years, I've had the opportunity to work with, lead, and be inspired by some of the most intelligent, capable, and challenging people I've ever known. Together, we were able to build teams that not only delivered extraordinary value but also became a brand. As a result, many of those people are now leaders of risk, analytics, product, and operations teams in various new startups and companies.

I'd like to thank the people who have mentored and helped me through my career. There are so many who've inspired and helped—too many to count—but I will still try to recognize at least some of them. Saar Wilf and Shvat Shaked for starting FraudSciences and Noam Naveh for being a great trainer and manager. Denise Aptekar, Dan Levy, Rohan Mahadevan, Elena Krasnoperova, and Alyssa Cutright for their mentorship through FraudSciences' acquisition and integration while they served as PayPal's risk leadership team. Tel Kedar and Chandra Narayanan for being inspiring and challenging peers. My brother Yuval Samet for being a strong business partner as we started and ran Analyzd together. Sebastian Siemiatkowski, Niklas Adalberth, and Victor Jacobsson, Klarna's founders, for being such great partners post-acquisition. And last but not least, my mentor, the late David Davidi, for his ongoing support and street smarts as I was paving my way. May he rest in peace.

PART I

Background and Theory

CHAPTER 1

What Is Risk Management in Payments?

Risk management in payments is a peculiar practice. Generally, risk management is focused on the analysis and reduction of risk in various types of activities. Specifically, it regards analysis (in its simplest definition: understanding a problem by dividing it into the smaller parts it is comprised of) of those activities, identification of potential risks (from operational through regulatory ones), and the design and implementation of controls in order to identify, understand, and mitigate those risks when they occur. As such, risk management in general can be and is carried out by business and policy analysts, dealing with the best way to impose controls on operating business units. The term *risk management* therefore refers to many parctices, most of them unrelated to the topic of this book. For ease of typing and reference, since this book only refers to risk management for online payments, hereafter I will use the acronym RMP.

Opposing my description of risk management as a supporting corporate function, RMP is a much more holistic activity. At its best, RMP includes several activities that broaden its scope significantly compared to what standard risk management means: it includes the actual operation of controls, monitoring and reporting of performance, product management for tools used in the implementation of those controls, and much more. It is also treated differently in various organizations, from being a part of Operations, through Finance, to a unit in its own right. When we joined PayPal, risk reported to the CTO; at Klarna, to the CEO. Accordingly, the heads of RMP in these teams vary from—most commonly—customer care professionals to financial analysts or, rarely, product people. All this creates confusion as to what RMP is and what it should be in charge of, as well as how we should think about its operation and performance.

Is RMP different when done for a retailer versus a payment provider or an issuer? In essence, no: all are dealing with similar fraudsters, in a similar space, and the range of tools and customer behaviors they see are similar. There are differences, though: losses are driven by different factors, since retailers mainly deal with consumers, and payment providers deal with both. Available data are different since retailers can see browsing patterns, and issuers don't know what the product is. Even the ability to react is different, since issuers can only block a card from transacting, but payment providers can block individual purchases or block a customer completely. Their ability to implement real-time detection, scale of available data, and tolerance to loss vary. Still, this book isn't separating retailers, issuers, and payment providers in any meaningful way. Historically, retailers could be slightly less concerned with cutting-edge technologies, since their margins were higher and a lot of their business was done offline. As many online businesses mature and start worrying more about margins, as well as increasingly become targeted by organized fraudsters, we see more convergence in the knowledge and tools required from all types of businesses.

There are two guiding principles to the way RMP should be thought of:

- **RMP is a core function of a payment organization.** Forcing your RMP team into Finance or Operations drives the team to look for solutions from a limited toolbox. If you are a RMP leader, you must be able to recognize and use trade-offs between rejections, losses, and cost of operation; therefore, RMP must be a separate, self-sufficient team that owns and impacts such trade-offs with input from the Sales team.

- **RMP is a data- and engineering-heavy activity.** RMP is not a human-intensive operational team aimed at reducing losses to a minimum using manual review. A substantial percentage of losses occurs due to operational, experience, and general product issues that should be managed with appropriate tools—not improved manual decisions by an ever-growing operations team. To deal with those, RMP teams must own product and data analysis responsibilities, creating substantially more value by independently identifying and fixing issues that would not be otherwise uncovered. Furthermore, day-to-day interaction with customers, together with the instrumentation (documenting and tracking events in your system and their impact on your data in a way that allows real-time and look-back analysis of actions taken) and tracking required for reporting losses and performance, adds to the team's competence to deal with systematic problems holistically. That also makes RMP teams the most qualified to come up with user-behavior-driven solutions that are otherwise hard to replicate.

The two guiding principles above dictate a specific structure and set of activities that should be carried out by the RMP team. This means that the team should be separate as a part of a data, analytics, or "data science" team. Setting the team up this way will not only drive higher success in controlling losses but also improve other value-creating activities that a data team can initiate and lead in your organization.

CHAPTER 2

What Problem(s) Are We Trying to Solve?

Actively going after further detection and analysis of problems, trends, and phenomena in your data and system is what drives the daily improvement that supports your strategy; it is a cycle where you identify your top issues, understand what causes them, and solve them so that other issues become your top concern. However, when you go after these issues, or when you find them, you need to deal with terminology;. How will you describe your findings? What is it that you're trying to solve?

We are trying to optimize our risk, according to our risk appetite, measured as a balance between our losses and rejections. Let's look at it step by step:

- **Optimizing risk.** Risk is determined by the probability of an adverse event happening (fraud chargeback, merchant going out of business, a renter's property being trashed) multiplied by the magnitude of damage we will incur (be it financial, reputational, or other).

- **According to our risk appetite.** Determining whether we're taking too much or too little risk is a decision owned by various officers of the company and/or external regulations—depending on the level and type of governance the company is subject to. The company's appetite determines the amount of risk it's willing to take; as any Head of RMP discovers, that appetite changes rapidly and is one of the major influences you must manage on a day-to-day basis. Regulation is a significant part of your risk appetite considerations. You will be regulated differently based on your business model, geography, volume, and license type. Some regulations and regulating bodies are more conservative than others, expecting certain types of decision models and style of decision making and documentation; others are open to reasonable explanations of innovative risk-taking models. All are concerned with what they understand as protecting consumers and businesses from various violations. This impacts the type of business decisions you are free to make.

- **Measured by losses and rejections.** The company is exposed to other costs and impacts due to adverse events; a bad reputation for being fraud ridden, as eBay used to have, is a good example. However, when dealing specifically with RMP, the most obvious numbers to track are loss rate—the total cost of chargebacks, disputes, defaults, and other penalties that we couldn't recoup from customers—and rejections—specifically, ones that were confirmed as false positives.

Optimizing Risk with a Solution-Based Approach

A proactive approach to risk management dictates repeatedly identifying risk factors, understanding them, and acting on them. Root cause analysis is a key process that allows the understanding needed to make sure you are using the right tools for the right problems. Root cause analysis is an iterative process: first isolate a sample of problematic cases, review a few of them to analyze what happened with each of them that led to loss to identify various types of loss causes, then split the sample into smaller groups until you have several subsamples, each driven by a specific combination of reasons causing loss (or any other problem you're trying to solve).

Root cause requires tracking an application's lifecycle step-by-step in order to understand exactly what happened to it. For example, if the cause of the problem isn't clear when looking at purchase details but the purchase had a dispute (I use *dispute* to describe customers contacting you to complain about a problem with your service, rather than talking to their bank or another third party) tied to it, you may interview the customer-care agent that dealt with it. You may track the type of emails or other messages sent to the customer to see if something got lost in translation or in delivery. You may check whether the package was actually delivered and whether the customer's signature was collected. This kind of deep investigation provides the best hints for detecting similar cases in the future and fixing the problems that caused them.

Let's say you have commerce activity in a few countries, and one day in August you look at your chargeback reports (a *chargeback* is a process that starts with a consumer disputing a credit card charge for fraud or bad service with their issuer, followed by your acquiring bank puling money from your account to compensate the consumer) and discover that you went from 0.2% in total chargeback volume to 0.4%. That's double the number, so obviously you're worried. What's going on? First you'll need to understand when the problem occurred. The fact that you got 0.4% in August doesn't mean a lot, because chargebacks come in at different times after the purchase. So you chart a graph by purchase date and discover that the bump stems from purchases made in April. What happened in April? Looking at incoming disputes you realize that complaints about nondelivery of goods peaked for purchases that month. It turns out that one of your suppliers was late and many customers got their products later than usual. Many complained and some gave up on the deal and charged back because customer-care staff was not properly briefed to give refunds. Loss? Indeed. Fraud? Not at all.

Consider another one: you work for a payments provider and your ops team reviews purchases and suddenly they notice multiple iPod purchases. That immediately seems suspicious, so you take a look at whether there's something connecting them. Quickly you discover that all of these purchases, although seemingly done by different people, were all done from the same IP at a computer lab at a university in Nevada. What's more, most of the people whose identity was used don't live anywhere close to Nevada, and it doesn't seem like their kids go there, either. One fraud attack on an electronics retailer averted!

A coherent and consistent framework or "risk language" must be used to describe the current state of affairs of your team's knowledge, assimilate new findings, and make sure that when a phenomenon is discussed using certain terms it is understood by everyone (analysts, modelers, developers, etc.) in a similar way. I've been using a relatively consistent framework through my years in RMP, and it has proven to cover most if not all phenomena while being sufficiently lightweight.

Why Talk About Loss and Not Fraud?

Fraud is a limiting definition causing us to look at the customer's intent as the root of all loss events. That is not the case. Misunderstanding, product issues, technical and process breakdowns, and general lack of financial planning can all lead to loss events. By looking at loss, we do not limit our thinking and investigative ability (this is why I choose to not use the term *friendly fraud* but rather *abuse* to describe some loss events). Customer behavior online is impacted by so many factors: your product features, the time of year, whether they had a little too much to drink and are aimlessly browsing the Web. They are often operating without malicious intent and, sometimes, without intent at all. The fact that they are sitting in front of a computer instead of physically interacting with a live human being impacts their mindset. They may have easier access to another's payment details at home or at work or just share a computer and not pay attention to who is logged in.

RMP domain experts must be able to understand a multidisciplinary collection of factors and processes that impact the eventual loss numbers, rather than look for malicious actions everywhere. This will also allow them to better cooperate with the revenue-creating side of your business. Losses have an impact on your margin not only by the money you lose but also as a result of the money you spend on risk activities; from direct cost for operations and data sources per purchase to investment in development of future models, risk is a cost center. Understanding that will help your team pay attention to their holistic impact on your business.

When data source usage is big, measuring overall spending on RMP activities is another important KPI (key performance indicator, the metrics you follow indicating your business' performance) to be measured and optimized. Data cost can reach the same level as losses and often much more, as could operational expenses on review staff. While this is an important aspect of the costs, this book is basic and only deals with the loss line.

CHAPTER 3

The Two Leading Approaches to the Analysis and Optimization of Losses

Once we understand what we're trying to achieve, we need to understand how we get there. How do we reduce the percentage of rejected customers and losses? There are two complementary approaches to this problem.

The Portfolio Approach

This approach looks at the company's portfolio of customers top down and looks for optimizations regardless of individual customers' behavior. This means that to reduce losses and rejections we need to provide an inflow of better customers—target safer industry segments, attract repeat consumers with lower risk profiles, etc., as well as block segments of ill-performing ones. If we need a shift in losses or rejections for a market or a large merchant, we can adjust our scoring threshold (which means a change to the trade-off between rejections and losses) to accept more or fewer consumers. Accordingly, this approach supports certain types of modeling and reporting that allow it to be effectively applied. The portfolio approach is most effective when dealing with long credit times: e.g., credit card, auto, and mortgage portfolios. This is because credit trends are local, sometimes hyperlocal, and are greatly impacted by macroeconomic trends not only for new applications (when I refer to principles relevant to both consumers and merchants, I use the term *application(s)*) but also in existing loans' due payments. The portfolio approach and its related modeling techniques have permeated from banking to RMP through companies like HNC/Fair Isaac and their alumni moving to PayPal, Amazon, and other large companies.

The Behavioral Approach

This approach looks at the company's business as a discrete series of interactions with customers and aims to make the right decision in every case based on correct classification of the customer's behavior. While there are different ways to go about doing so, they generally agree—if we have a problem with losses or rejections, we must identify trends and behaviors that drive that trend and solve its underlying reasons. This usually means case-by-case investigation and uncovering of "root causes" for losses and rejections, in an attempt to correctly classify wanted and unwanted phenomena.

Which of These Methods Works Better?

As I noted, they are complementary, with each fitting different circumstances. Both are highly effective when used correctly. The portfolio approach is especially effective when working in mature markets (where product issues and major problematic behaviors have been identified, modeled, and solved) and for dealing with macroeconomic risks (such as shifts in debt-to-income ratio due to high unemployment or targeting of a subprime population). The portfolio approach can also help guide a company's entrance to a new market: it is easier to set standards for what are "safe" industry segments to target and mid-market merchants to partner with than to predict individual behaviors when initially entering a market.

The behavioral approach is effective and needed when you deal with high-magnitude risks (e.g., sexual predator detection in chat rooms) or in cases where behaviors can change rapidly. In RMP, a large proportion of loss cases are a result of a malicious and planned action by a prepared adversary. Those patterns change rapidly in response to your actions and any weakness you may expose, since there is clear incentive for overcoming your defenses. In addition, unlike with long-term loans such as credit lines, every purchase or merchant on-boarding (*on-boarding* means deciding to accept the business as your customer) is a decision point. At that point, your decision or the user's behavior may change, allowing flexibility in response from both sides;

the portfolio approach is limited at dealing with such threats. Therefore, to deal with fraud, abuse, and nascent markets, one must be able to use the behavioral approach, while for mature markets and credit decisions, you must be able to use the portfolio approach to make top-down trade-offs.

CHAPTER 4

How Should We Describe and Understand Behavior?

Through our interaction with our customers (I am using *consumers* to indicated the individual making a purchase or a payment, *merchants* to indicate the providers of goods or receivers of payments, and *customers* to indicate both), from first encounter to termination, we see changes in the details they provide us, how they act on our website, their interaction with us through email and phone, and much more. We constantly re-evaluate our customers at any of these points to see if there are any alarming changes that require our attention. How do we make sense of them? By using them to answer three questions:

1. **Who is this?** Our interaction with our customers—whether they make a purchase, start using a service, or call customer care—starts with a simple assertion of identity. There are two things to establish here:

   a. **Validation:** Does person X or company Y really exist? Dealing with a nonexistent entity (person or company) exposes you to multiple problems, from simple fraud (as a company, I sell products but never ship them) to money laundering. That is why companies are subject to KYC/KYB regulations (Know Your Customer/Know Your Business, a set of regulations defining the minimal set of information to collect about your customers). Still, even for unregulated companies, being able to make sure that your customer's identity is valid and exists in the world is basic.

b. **Authorization and Authentication:** Establishing that someone or something exists is one thing. The other question is
whether the person currently claiming to be X or Y is indeed
that person, or someone authorized by that person/company
to act on their behalf. An authorized person may be a family
member, a friend, or a co-worker, not necessarily the person
whose details they provide—but nonetheless they need to be
authenticated (have the right credentials) and authorized (have
permission to use those credentials). Failing to check that exposes your system to the use of stolen identities by both fraudsters and relatives. In addition, if you offer password-protected
accounts, your accounts will be targeted for hacking (since it's
easier to steal a password for an established account than fake
one). If you manage a marketplace, having one of your trusted
merchants' accounts hacked and maliciously used to sell non-
existing inventory is highly unpleasant and creates loss that's
hard to recover. While difficult, users' needs (parents letting
kids use their account, multiple employees using a single account, or MMO players buying "power leveling" services) dictate that you must be able to identify authorized and unau-
thorized uses of the same identity by multiple people.

2. **Can they keep their commitment?** The question of financial and
operational ability is the one most debated in credit modeling and
less so when dealing with fraud and "classic" RMP for eCommerce. Failure to address this question exposes you to customers
taking on financial commitments for extended periods of time,
some of them in good will, and then defaulting. While consumers
may not be getting a credit line from you, merchants essentially
are. If they presell a large amount of stock and get defrauded into
bankruptcy by a supplier, fail to provide adequate customer care
and provide defective products, or fraudulently sell something
they don't intend to ship, you are exposed for the whole sum. Most
probably you are going to pay at least some, if not all, of the pro-
ceeds to your merchant—and be left with the complaints when
they disappear. You should also think of any situation in which
you are effectively fronting a customer money by paying them in
advance of having money in your bank account as credit granting.
If you enable same-day direct bank payments without ensuring
positive balance in customers' account, you are in fact extending
credit. Since customers' ability to keep their commitment is un-
dertreated in many RMP teams and most of the knowledge about

merchant credit is from banking (and therefore not easily adjusted for online or contemporary business needs), merchant-driven losses are constantly on the rise. Looking at customers' ability should be twofold: what they can afford now as well as what they will be able to afford in the future; whether their ability to pay is stable. This is true to consumers getting a long-term loan and also to merchants whose financial standings can deteriorate.

3. **Will they keep their commitment?** Customers can be who they say they are and also capable of fulfilling on their commitments but never intend to do so. Since the online experience is not a personal one (online businesses look for scale, which is contrary to personal 1:1 communication) the psychological barrier to fraud, or just neglect to pay or communicate properly, is much lower. As a result, customers are not adverse to having late payments, false charge-backs, and other unfounded claims. Serial abusers will identify a way to reduce their liability and get away with a certain behavior and will do so repeatedly unless detected and stopped. Therefore, being able to either detect good intent or impact customers' mindset to want to keep their commitments is another component of a RMP system.

Remember: People Make Mistakes

A lot of the loss you deal with, up to mid-double digits, can be caused by various mistakes made by employees or customers. Of course you may see cases of customers claiming to not understand something about your product as an excuse for not paying or even experience employee fraud, but more often than not there are genuine, large-scale problems in your product, experience, or operations that cause losses. Whenever you look into a loss case, you must first rule out any of those.

Your product may drive losses by the way it works. This comes into play when customers fail to understand features they are buying, or that in fact they are buying something. If your user acquisition is based on a free sample followed by automatic registration or a change of cost, some of your customers will end up being unable to pay or just uninterested in paying. These could be built into your product and be considered a cost of doing business and will be almost impossible to detect in advance.

Your customer experience can drive losses. Disputes are an example: if a consumer tries to submit a legitimate dispute about a merchant and has a hard time going through your dispute flow, you will be slapped with an unnecessary chargeback and additional fees for a case that could have ended with a refund. Another simple example is your dynamic descriptor, the text that appears next to your charge in the credit card's statement; if that is unclear or hard to search and identify, you will see unjustified chargebacks.

Operational issues may also cause losses. Multiple problems can be caused by money movement just being complicated, but also from relying on increasingly old and malfunctioning financial systems. Corruption of the acquirer's settlement file, the file contains the payments it captured (actually debited) for you, could lead to some payments being incorrectly allocated and appearing as losses when they're not supposed to; the same can happen with internal accounting allocation of payment revenues. Wrong procedures in dispute handling may cause wrong settlements in either side's favor that are inconsistent with your protection policy—driving angry merchants to not pay their fees and leave your platform—or just drive consumers to issue more chargebacks.

People makes mistakes, and that's part of every day life in your business. Those mistakes can many times be fixed easily (by a change in procedure or text in an email) and make a big difference in your losses. Always take that into consideration when you analyze root cause, because assuming intentful actions by customers may often lead you to the wrong conclusions.

Putting the Framework to Use

Using the three questions (Who are they? Can they meet their obligations? Will they?), we can explain and describe most loss occurrences. While theoretically these questions are mutually exclusive and describe the majority of phenomena we'll run across, we must remember that:

1. The indicators we collect from our users will not point at one or the other in a mutually exclusive manner. Does a consumer providing slightly altered details show bad will, stolen identity, or simply privacy awareness? If a consumer tries to shop, gets rejected, and then tries again for a lower amount, is this lack of finances

or abusive behavior? Even if a negative event occurred and loss has materialized, it's often hard to distinguish what the absolutely real cause for it has been.

2. People make mistakes. A lot of the theory and many policies assume that customers' actions are a reaction to something (even if not rational, such as the feeling that they don't need to pay a virtual service because it's a victimless crime). The truth, however, is more complicated. If you do your work well, big shifts in your actual losses will be driven by major events (big new merchant introducing a completely different population, macroeconomic shifts, a new product). On a day-to-day level, though, the majority of losses will be driven by mistakes. These causes can be detected and eliminated by root cause analysis but are not covered by the above framework.

Putting aside integration issues, as discussed, customer behavior should all fit into this matrix. Most of your customers in a standard eCommerce operation will be who they say they are (own the identity they're using) as well as have the money and the willingness to pay. They are the people shopping from work or home, providing their own payment details, and are unlikely to charge back unless there's a huge issue with your service.

Most of the fraud you'll see is at the other side of the spectrum: perpetrated by fraudsters who use stolen or fake identities and do not have an intent to pay. In most cases, however, they (or rather the person who's details they stole) will have the funds to pay—if the card they're using doesn't have any balance on it, their purchase won't go through, and therefore fraudsters will not be interested in their cards; that means that any detection mechanism aimed at figuring out whether there's money in one's account is not going to help detect most blatant fraud.

A third example is abuse, sometimes referred to as *friendly fraud*. As noted previously, cases of "borrowed" identity (the person expected to pay is related to the person initiating the purchase, as in cases in which children use their parents' card details) are not really fraud: there's ability to pay and the identity was not stolen, but the willingness to pay is missing. This is a unique type of behavior, where the "borrower" feels that nonpayment online is a victimless crime or maybe that the use of the Internet's semi-anonymity allows different behavior than when face to face (some consumers almost treat online fraud as the equivalent of stealing cash from their parents' wallet). Fraud is about identity theft and forging details, and abusers should be treated as misguided individuals who are lax on personal standards but will behave well when reminded. A vast body of research repeatedly demonstrates how this works in real life.

As you can see, there is a vast range of behaviors for both consumers and merchants to understand and work with, and detecting them is both science and art. Being able to detect, analyze root cause, and then act on major problems and emerging trends is the core of what the RMP team should do day to day. Now that we've established basic terminology, we are free to discuss the topics that build on it.

PART II

Organization and People

CHAPTER 5

The Goals and Functions of a Payments Risk Management Team

What Does a Payments Risk Management Organization Do?

Every organization is different in its setup, the types of people it has, and its historical constraints. This is why I'm focusing on a list of functions that the RMP team should be in charge of and contain, as well as the relationships between those functions, rather than who reports to whom. In describing these functions, I think of a RMP team that deals with a wide array of problems: merchant on-boarding, fraud, abuse, credit issues, and more. As you decide to focus on specific domains, you can trim and only use some of these functions; however, all of them should exist to some degree, even if your problem domain is more limited.

A RMP team needs to be able to quickly identify threats and loss drivers, quantify and understand their origins, and use or develop tools that will allow it to manage those threats while monitoring them. It needs to be able to cater to its own needs quite independently because it has unique needs and because standard development cycles don't work well with the ever-changing landscape of user behavior. Finally, it needs to grow and foster domain expertise, making sure that it is documented and shared across the organization.

In its broadest form, a RMP team should contain several functions: Operations, Decision Automation, Analytics, and Product.

Payment Risk Operations: Making Sure You Run Smoothly

Operations is the team in charge of day-to-day work. It is the one dealing with customers, using a set of tools to detect trends and provide stop-gap solutions. Ops is the gateway to your organization. This is the team into which you can hire inexperienced employees, train them, test them on the job, and promote them if they show talent. This is where domain experts grow, but the bulk of its work is making sure that behaviors that get past your automatic systems are detected, reviewed, understood, and dealt with. Its main delivery is loss and false positive prevention through various manual decisons (since we're trying to predict and prevent a loss-causing event, a false positive here is an application wrongly classified as "bad" and rejected). Accordingly, it is measured not only by prevented losses but also decision accuracy, speed, efficiency per decision analyst, and response time to detected trends.

Operations contains various subfunctions that have different expertise:

- **Consumer and Merchant Risk Ops** are the two functions in charge of tracking and making manual decisions regarding your customers: underwriting, placing and releasing limitations on their activities, etc. These functions provide insightful root cause analysis and serve as domain experts for automation purposes. They are the ones that are operating detection tools and responding to alerts, and they operate both on application (purchase, onboarding) and through the customer's lifecycle.

- **Fraud Prevention Support** serves as RMP's link to the world. Answering customers' questions about possible and actual fraud cases, working with your company's legal department and law enforcement agencies (submitting Suspicious Activity Reports in the US or their equivalents worldwide, enforcing Anti Money Laundering controls), and investigating fraud rings. This is not a customer-service function although it may serve as a place to which senior customer-service agents can advance; at times, they should serve as third- or fourth-line support for incoming inquiries—since this function's expertise is understanding and communicating fraud activity and getting external stakeholders to assist your company in preventing them.

- **The Recovery Team** (in consumer lending, sometimes called *Collections* or *Credit Operations*) is involved with recovering losses from customers who don't pay. A lot of discussion about RMP is focused on quick and accurate decisions at the time of purchase or when on-boarding a merchant; in fact, strong chargeback management firms demonstrate 60%–70% success rates in recovering chargebacks after those have been filed, and Collection teams report success rates (in canceling chargebacks) of up to 95%, depending on geography. This is the function's responsibility—by calling, emailing, and mailing customers, by challenging chargebacks with the acquirer, and sometimes by taking legal action, this function is measured by its ability to get you money that you thought was lost.

Decision Automation: Allowing You to Scale

The Decision Automation function deals with creating, maintaining, and improving automated decision and decision support systems. This includes models, feature engineering (the important processes of hypothesizing, designing, testing, and using the indicators (features) for the type of behavior we want to detect), and additional detection systems. In addition to modeling, this function should be in charge of most of the prototyping activity in the team: new tools for Ops, linking and velocity systems, and alternative data sources. It is also expected to be actively involved in data infrastructure and delivery, working with DBAs (database administrators, in charge of managing your data infrastructure—making sure it is up and working properly), or implementing a data warehouse (a database optimized for analysis and reporting rather than for reading and writing speed, a common requirement for production databases). As such, it must have some rudimentary engineering capability of its own in addition to working closely with (or including) the engineers in charge of RMP's production code. This function has the biggest impact on your team's major KPIs—losses and rejection rate—and should be measured accordingly.

Analytics: Making Sure You Know What's Going On

The Analytics function is your top-down eye on what's happening in your portfolio, looking at it from various dimensions. This is the function into which you'd hire Finance folks and MBAs, and indeed, in some organizations, its function sits within Finance. Analytics is the function that measures, analyzes, and presents your KPIs and performance, and it's expected to identify trends and their drivers in an accurate and timely manner while making correct projections. Its major responsibilities are reporting current performance, forecasting future performance (and adjusting your provision—the funds you reserve on your income statement to offset future losses), and anticipating portfolio behavior development based on purchase inflow.

Product Management: Bridging a Rather Narrow Gap

The Product function is a rather established one and doesn't require introduction. What's important to understand is where it fits into the RMP team. Domain experts working with engineers on automation serve as product owners of sorts and do not require product support. Product managers are required, though, and they should focus on three areas:

- **Internal tools:** Due to the complexity of the job and general lack of suitable tools, product is required to lead the work to develop new tools or adapt off-the-shelf tools, according to ever-changing needs. Review tools tend to have many distinct use cases, and they change rapidly; being able to generalize and use development resources wisely is important.

- **Data and decision infrastructure:** Either off-the-shelf (rare) or home grown, data delivery (fetching and summarizing external and internal data for decision use) and decision infrastructure (real-time models) need to be developed and integrated. While seemingly a straightforward task, often this is complicated due to performance (on the decision side) and regulation (privacy, access control, and discrimination on the data-source side). As a result, being integrated properly to data sources and decision systems that work well for various countries is a strong competitive advantage and barrier to new entrants.

- **Customer interaction:** RMP teams often focus on real-time detection and some after-the-fact processing of claims. There is a whole world of opportunity in customer interaction that can help curb losses and improve customer satisfaction. From front-end authentication flows that challenge suspicious users to prove their identity to automated dispute flows, a savvy product team has to tackle the design and optimization of user interaction.

CHAPTER 6

Hiring for Your RMP Team

How do you start a RMP team? How big should it be? When do you hire engineers, statisticians, and others? These are very common questions when approaching RMP for the first time. Even for experienced risk managers, the question of the ideal employee profile still stands. How do you build the team?

When discussing hiring, I constantly emphasize the need for domain experts. By that, I refer to people who understand the customers' behaviors, needs, and their results both generally for the industry and specifically for your business. They have deep understanding of what this book is about—detecting, analyzing, and solving loss-causing problems. Most importantly, their understanding is anchored in actual work experience, having looked at and solved a large number of problems over a long period of time. Domain experts can be hired with experience, but a large number of them will grow in your organization, as they learn through operating your product and talking to customers.

Some Important Comparison Points

Every team is slightly different, but the following metrics are the most common and should drive your team composition:

- Your eventual loss rate should be determined by your business model. For most online businesses using credit card, that's under 1% across your portfolio.

- Your review rate—the percent of purchases your team manually reviews—should be under 1% for matured segments and markets, and no more than 30% for new ones. If you aren't close to these numbers, your automation effort is falling behind.

- An individual reviewer should reach 100–200 reviews a day, depending on the type of cases they review. If you are not close to this number, your tools and procedures are lacking.

- One decision-automation analyst can process insights from four or five review agents. You may need more analysts to support your general analytics activities. If you need more than this proportion, either your data availability is bad and requires a lot of manual work from the analysts to gain access or your analysts are not technical enough to overcome simple technical and analysis automation issues (which could be as simple as removing all non-alphanumeric characters from a long list of phone numbers or splitting email addresses to username and domain).

- One analyst can provide insights and feature requests to keep two or three engineers busy. If more engineers are needed, you may have an engineering efficiency issue. Since risk code is often in the core of any legacy code, this is quite common.

If you run an established team and find that you are operating at completely different levels, you may have a unique business model and way of operation; however, most likely you are suffering from one of the issues I noted above or others. Fix them before throwing more bodies at the problem, as more people compound operational and infrastructure problems in the long run rather than solve them.

What If I Don't Have Anyone?

If you are just starting, you should start with two people: an operator and an engineer. The operator's role is to be the first of your review staff, and one that will evolve to be a domain expert and an analyst with time. Taking this approach guarantees that the person in charge of automation will understand the ins and outs of your business before moving to develop rules and flows for it. The operator needs to work for about 6 months in full capacity—hire additional people if needed —before you hire the first engineer. The engineer doesn't have to be a machine learning expert—actually, it is preferable not to hire one at this stage—because most of the work is going to be infrastructure and incremental work on developing features for detection. What this person does need to have is good understanding of data and how to structure and store it for future analysis as well as some product grasp to be able to work with the operators, who will have a hard time articulating their needs at first. With time, the operations team will grow while the more senior people will become decision-automation analysts, and the engineering team will expand to additional practices. Most teams do not need statisticians and machine learning experts before a whole year has passed.

Hiring Your First Operator

While hiring engineers is a highly debated practice, hiring operators is not as much. There are some experienced operators in payments, but the requirement to grow into analysts and participate in decision automation is often beyond what most operational people are willing to take on. How do you find the right people for this team?

- No other area is as ripe for hiring young talent and getting them on-the-job training as RMP. You can provide these people with a structured development process that will benefit your whole team, while reducing your need for experienced talent.

- Look for people with basic technical understanding and some statistical intuition; some, but probably not all, of your customer-care team members demonstrate this capability, and some can grow into Recovery/Fraud Support roles. Your domain experts must be able to generalize on trends they identify and translate them into features and rules at a reasonable level; you can test for that by asking candidates to devise ways to steal from you. The answers may surprise you.

- Balance well between quants and team members from diverse backgrounds. Quants do a great job building models but often not a good job in identifying and articulating phenomena, especially in corner cases or small numbers of occurrences that require a lot of assumptions and some intuition to connect the dots and explain a customer's behavior. Social sciences and Humanities graduates will contribute to this aspect of your team. Some of my best hires were majors in music, theatre, psychology, and biology; that is what allowed us to, for example, build a repeat-offender system modeled after virus behavior and an analytic method based on sociological and criminological elements.

- Try to hire engineering talent into your operational team, and do so early; hire ex-engineers looking to make a change into operational roles in the Consumer/Merchant risk Ops teams.

PART III

Tools and Methods

CHAPTER 7

Detection: Figuring Out that Something Is Wrong

Detecting that "something" is happening in your system is one of the core activities of the RMP team. How do you set up effective detection mechanisms? By employing three activities: measuring your current performance, using inflow to predict future performance, and setting up mechanisms to detect outlier activity that needs to be investigated.

Measuring Performance

The biggest advantage in measuring your performance based on actual numbers is being able to know exactly what's going on. The biggest disadvantage is that you have to wait a long time to get that number, basically making it impossible to respond to events in any reasonable amount of time; you could be out of business by the time you get your fully developed loss numbers. While measuring your rejection rate (the percent of stopped applications at every stage of your decision process [models, manual decisions]) is pretty straightforward, merely trying to understand which of your rejections is a mistake is going to take a while. As I noted before, card payment originating time based cohorts take 60–70 days to reach 95% development, which means that it takes several months to get to around 95% of chargebacks you can expect to receive for this cohort. In consumer lending, write-off time (the point in a debt's lifecycle when you stop collecting and declare a debt lost and off your balance sheet) is based on your payment terms and the way regulation defines default—most probably a much longer time.

Measuring performance as well as understanding it requires that you understand the different steps in your value chain as well as have an overall view; optimization doesn't only mean losses vs. rejections but can also include collection cost and revenue. Your recovery activity economics (the cost for challenging a chargeback, your ability to charge a late fee, etc.) may change your risk appetite and tolerance toward some people not paying you initially. Your current and estimated loss rates determine whether you can operate profitably, enter a market more aggressively, or need to make quick actions to limit a growing problem.

Measuring Offset Performance: Time-Based Cohorts

One of the basic yet important things to remember when measuring performance is understaing that the performance you see today is not a result of decisions you made yesterday, but rather a longer period of time ago. This is where time-based cohorts come in handy. Time-based cohorts mean that you present results, such as loss rates, based on when applications were received rather than when you learned of the loss, e.g., all credit card purchases attempted in a certain month. The correct or incorrect decisions you made on an application are a result of your detection capability and understanding at the time it was attempted, not the time at which you discovered a problem, since that could be anywhere from a few seconds to a few months after approval. If you received five chargebacks today, you cannot infer that you made five bad decisions yesterday. Maybe one chargeback is for a month-old purchase, and the other is for a week-old one. You must look at the originating cohort, the time frame these purchases were approved on, to analyze whether you have a problem relative to other purchases in that cohort.

What Should You Measure?

Measure Your Defaults

A default happens when people don't pay when they're supposed to or charge back on a payment. It doesn't mean that you won't recover some or all of that debt later, but it does mean that you'll have to work for it. Defaulted volume is sometimes referred to as *gross loss*; after all recovery steps, when written off, it is sometimes referred to as *net loss*.

When measuring consumer defaults, in addition to measuring totals (number of defaults, their volume, and percent of total payments volume) you should at least group by product (if you have more than one), by payment instrument (direct bank payment vs. Visa vs. Amex vs. other payment options), and by the way in which you found out about the default (chargeback, customer complaint, analyst flagging, etc.). Different products and default-discovery channels work differently, have different false-positive rates, draw a different mix of consumers, have different collection success rates down the line, and so on. You must segment to be able to track different populations effectively.

Another important dimension is industry segment. This is true for both consumer and merchant defaults and is driven by portfolio risk management. Macroeconomic changes leading to lower consumption, credit shortage impacting high amount, high cash-flow-dependent segments, or a sales team too focused on risky segments can quickly turn your portfolio south without you noticing. Bad merchants bring in worse customers and tend to default more themselves.

When you measure your performance this way, you must again deal with the fact that defaults take a while to mature; while you care about gross loss, net loss is what you usually optimize for (while taking recovery cost/benefit into consideration). Suppose you're looking at all purchases from last month. How do you know what their eventual loss rate is going to look like, whether you're improving or worsening, and what drives those trends? Part of the answer is measuring and inferring based on inflow—the topic of our next section—but by comparing early loss evolution you can try to infer what future performance will look like. Looking at loss evolution[1] at different points in time (5, 10, 20, 30, or so days after purchase until you hit your write-off point) and comparing how different cohorts are doing will allow you to identify problematic cohorts and assess what their future performance is going to look like.

Measure Your Recovery

Loss optimization can be driven by measuring defaults, but that needs to be complemented by other numbers. Specifically, for problems with ability to pay—credit issues—but also with intent problems, recovery

---

1. A way to describe how your time-based origination cohorts are doing over time. It plots portfolio default level for a certain cohort at different, but set, points in time, for comparison.

and the way you manage it can make the difference between a losing and profitable operation. You must track recovery cost and success.

Your main KPIs should be recovery success rate (as simple as percent of net loss from gross loss), average number and cost of actions done on each default, and the success rate of every action: both in being able to reach the defaulted party and driving for full or partial payment of the debt. Different financial institutions may handle chargeback management differently, have easier or harder decision processes, and generally impose different success rates on your operations. Make it a priority to identify vendors that make it harder to recover. As in any other case, you should always perform A/B tests. Much as in any customer-facing activity, A/B testing helps to improve performance. A/B testing here means designing experiments to test competing services against one another on similar populations, then choosing the ones producing the best results. Collection agencies work differently in different regions, have different modeling techniques and cost structures, and may prove to have highly varying efficiency. The same is relevant for external chargeback management; due to different unit economics they may end up optimizing against you.

Any relationship with a vendor can be plagued with conflicts of interest. However, in payments it is undeniably evident with every purchase. Specifically regarding loss liability, the hot potato lands way too often in the retailer's lap. If you use PayPal, for example, different products will have different protection policies, meaning that you may end up with vastly different loss levels, even with identical default levels.

Measure Your Rejections

Rejections should be analyzed not only because they are lost revenue —some consumers will try again until successful, some are rejected due to system errors and data malfunctions, some just type their information incorrectly. Rejections happen for many reasons, and their analysis helps discover product and flow issues.

- **Instrumentation.** Proper instrumentation will provide you with enough data to conduct in-depth analysis and determine the reasons for a rejection. Rejections should be instrumented and logged in exactly the same way as approved applications: data content, time stamp, decisions, and so on. Rejections should also have a trace of all systems that recommended a rejection, not only the one that actually rejected them. This will allow the creation of what-if scenarios—simulating what additional volume of approved applications will enter the system if a detection system is altered.

- **Control Groups.** If you apply a certain rejection to 100% of a certain population, you have no way of knowing whether a behavior shifted, was eliminated, or was misinterpreted by your system. Allowing a reasonably sized control group depends on your portfolio size and distribution and system structure, but it is a tool you have to implement and use from the get go or you will always have to hack something to compensate for not having one. Three to six months down the line from layering detection systems without a control group, you will have no clue why a customer was denied. Thus, you need to measure your rejections' real performance and false positives against the control group to get a clear picture.

Defining a Rejection. What's a rejected customer in your flow? How should you calculate rejection rate? Should all customers be accepted on their first try? Is an application that you challenge with questions and accept the same as an application you accept up front? Measuring raw rejection rate (where every rejection counts) is advisable but requires that you know, in detail, the reasons for each rejection, or you're at risk of trying to optimize on model rejections when most of your problems are, maybe, faulty merchant integrations. Measuring "cleaned" rejection rates (where, for example, a consumer that tried more than once and eventually got accepted is not considered to be rejected) makes sense when you don't have that level of accuracy, but should be accompanied by an analysis of how repeated rejections and tries impact customer LifeTime Value (LTV).

Measure Ops Performance

Payments risk operations are your last line of defense on defaults, and the Recovery team is the one saving you from write-offs. You need to know how these teams perform as a group and as individuals to make sure that you are investing in the right tools and people. While defaults and recovery are covered in previous bullets, here I'm referring to measuring the efficiency and efficacy of the teams' operation.

Although you should not staff your team with strictly customer-service-oriented personnel, Ops should still be measured for responsiveness, throughput, and accuracy of decisions or recovery attempts. Manual actions must be automated away using flow-management tools, and data collection actions should be done automatically—APIs have become very popular, and programatic data access is very common. A word of clarification: I refer to customer-service professionals and where I see them fit in the RMP team. In determining that most customer-service-trained staff shouldn't double as your manual decision team, I'm using the term "customer service" very broadly, referring to staff focused on interacting with and helping customers vs. analytically and/or technically inclined people. Of course, many talented people can do both, but promoting from within customer service will usually find professionals who are much more focused on the former rather than the latter. Thier talents are highly needed in the support and recovery teams.

There are two main differences between a customer-care team and risk ops.

The first is that process quality can be measured and optimized on much more than customer interaction quality. You should be able to measure and improve the number of cases that are sent to Ops and their quality, the effectiveness of the decision process (number of clicks to decision, average number of data sources used per decision, number of opened tabs), and the analyst's ability to decide (from average time per decision crossed with accuracy, to the probability of that agent asking for more information or deferring to a senior agent before making a decision).

The second difference is that tying individuals' and teams' performance to actual quantitative data, rather than just qualitative, is easier. It is relatively easy, and must be one of your core measuring activities, to see how much your Ops and Recovery activities are saving your company. For Consumer Risk Ops, for example, measure rejected volume, discounted by what they reject incorrectly or miss. For the Recovery team, measure the conversion of defaults to write-offs on a per-purchase basis. You'd be surprised to find out that the best recovery agents can be 10x better than the worst ones on a per-action basis.

I am delivering a two-sided message in this book: on one hand, use Ops extensively; on the other hand, use them in a specific manner. A huge part of using Ops as domain experts is delivering the right quality of cases, the complicated and ambiguous ones, rather than clear-cut cases that can be automatically sorted. The main indicator of case quality is review queue hit rate: how many of those purchases put in the review queue are actually bad, based on whether the team rejected them or not.

What's "Normal" Performance?

How do you know if you're doing a good job? What performance numbers do you need to aspire to? Defaults, rejections, and operations performance depend on your industry, type of payment, country, and loss tolerance, and they vary accordingly. Still, the following are some numbers that are important as reference.

Defaults

For most businesses operating in the US and using credit cards, 1% is the upper limit, with most hovering around 0.4% for purely online purchases. Lending businesses working with prime customers perform very close to their respective country's credit card defaults; many Western countries are at around 6%. Subprime lending sees defaults in the low 20s or high 10s. These are numbers for your whole portfolio. You may be very tolerant toward losses in new markets or some products—some digital merchants are fine with 5%–15% loss rates, and they refund payments upon first complaint. While these may be standard numbers, they are definitely not optimal. FraudSciences had less than 0.1% losses in high-risk payments, Klarna reports <1% losses while granting short-term credit, and PayPal reported not more than 0.26% of losses while covering more and more of its merchant base's losses.

Rejections

As the flip side of losses, rejection numbers are both complicated to discern and not shared publicly. Businesses using credit cards in the US have rejection rates that reach a maximum of 5% and go as low as 0.5%. Lending businesses can go up to 80% rejection, depending on the credit status of their customer base. Roughly speaking, rejection rates of more than 10% are high for any standard online business using cards or bank transfers without providing any loss guarantee. Klarna reports less than 10% rejections as a lending business; FraudSciences gave a loss guarantee, took high-risk purchases, and had a 25% rejection rate.

Operations Performance

Review time and effectiveness differ significantly between industries and rely on automation, data, and tool quality. As you increase automation, review time actually becomes longer, since review staff get more complicated cases. Still, five-minute reviews are reasonable, with one-minute reviews for first-tier simple cases being the goal. False positives at this stage could go up to 20%.

Detecting that "Something" Is Happening

Detection efforts deal with two issues. The first is detecting phenomena that you expect to happen in your system: some types of fraud, abusive behavior, or maybe a positive trend. The other is being able to understand when an unexplained phenomenon, one that may or may not lead to losses and increased risk, is occurring in your system. While measuring performance in its early or late stages can point to an existing problem, detecting trends early can lead to those losses being prevented. Let's look at a few ways to detect issues in advance.

Incoming Complaints

Closely monitoring suspicious cases flagged by consumers, merchants, and employees is one of the major data sources for your detection efforts. Consumers suddenly starting to complain about a merchant, higher levels of nonshipment complaints, or a merchant pointing at a trend they see on their website—all are possible leads for a trend you may have missed.

Inflow

One portfolio-level indicator for a change in your risk levels is your application inflow, and more accurately inflow composition. This means looking at the types of applications you're getting and checking whether that has changed compared to historical trends, even before seeing a single default. Different consumers and merchants have different risk profiles, and understanding that you are seeing a different population than the one you were used to is a leading indicator for trouble (or, sometimes, very good news). There are many ways to attack portfolio segmentation for inflow measurement; however, some are more common.

If you are already deploying real-time models, measuring score or classification distribution shift in accepted and rejected applications is the first one; since your score is an indication of the risk level you assign to customers; as long as your model's performance hasn't deteriorated significantly, a shift in score distribution (for example: more consumers accepted at low scores than expected) can signal issues.

What's a score distribution, and what does a shift mean? Your model assigns a score to each application. Normally, you'd expect these scores to show normal distribution, peaking around the threshold score. If you plot scores given by the model for a certain cohort and see that suddenly you have an over-representation of higher or lower scores than usual (to put it more plainly, the curve shifted and peaks at a different score, or has multiple peaks), this is an indication of a shift in your population.

In addition to scores, you should segment inflow based on (at least) product type, age group, amount (in case of purchases), and industry segment. If one of these subsegments becomes more prominent in its contribution to overall volume, it needs to be looked into. A higher than average purchase volume from 18–22 year olds in the clothing segment could mean that summer sales are coming, but also that you have a new merchant drawing young shoppers with significantly lower prices—increasing their operational risk—or any number of other reasons.

Linking

Fraud only matters when done at scale. Fraudsters and most abusers aren't just looking to get away with one free item or service; they are in the business of stealing valuables and reselling them. Being a fraudster requires investment: time, purchase of stolen identities or hacked accounts, setting up proxies, finding drop addresses, or more plainly the risk of getting caught. If they cannot effectively repeat their actions and steal a lot of value from you or your merchants, their return on investment is too low, and that alone will deter most of them. Therefore, limiting scale—limiting the ability to repeatedly exploit a weakness in your system in a similar fashion over time—is one of the things you have to pay close attention to.

Linking is mostly concerned with horizontal scale, the fraudsters' tendency to find a loophole in your system, then repeat it as often as possible using multiple identities and customer accounts that are supposed to seem unrelated. Linking, therefore, is a mechanism used to connect customers and their activities together so you can detect when they come back, and especially when they come back while manipulating their details and trying to hide from your regular detection efforts and look like a completely new or unrelated user.

Implementing a linking mechanism can be very simple or highly complex. The simplest implementation requires nothing more than explicit matching between two purchases or accounts to deem them linked. Still, even when using simple linking heuristics you need to be able to filter: only linking using IP, even if explicit, will result in many false-positive links, such as multiple customers using one workplace's network. You therefore need to combine a few assets as links.

Some Linking Terminology

An explicit link means that details in two purchases are identical, e.g., both applications come from the same IP or email.

A fuzzy link is any link that involves partial similarity. Two accounts using IPs 111.bbb.aaa.1 and 111.bbb.aaa.2 can be related since they share a c-class from an uncommon network.

As with any type of behavior, patterns in linking can point to specific behaviors, some riskier than others. Most commonly, if two purchases come from the same IP and email but not the same name and address, they are highly suspicious. Most of the times this linking pattern is pointing to a fraudster using multiple identities in various purchases.

How Complex Should Your Linking Be?

Creating more sophisticated linking can be done by (1) collecting more data or those that are hard(er) to obfuscate (such as new types of cookies), (2) adding fuzzy matching, and (3) recursive matching, going beyond one level of matching on a smaller set of assets. There's always more data to be collected and fuzzy matching to be done, but returns diminish quickly after the first few basic link types. That is why most companies offering linking as a service are struggling. Developing something simple in-house captures most of the benefit. Recursive matching refers to linking starting from a base entity A and returning not only the $B_{1..i}$ entities linked to it directly but also the $C_{1..i}$ entities linked to B-class entities, up to the Nth level. This is done because fraudsters, even the more-sophisticated ones, tend to reuse assets. That is also the reason why more data have quickly diminishing returns.

The biggest issue with linking isn't algorithm complexity but implementation, especially for real-time linking on large data sets. Creating a fully fledged linking mechanism that works close to real-time is a big investment—fuzzy linking is especially tasking on whatever data infrastructure you use—and thus hard to justify. As a result, finding the optimal functionality to deploy in real-time is a complex exercise in ROI calculation.

Velocity

While measuring inflow allows you to see changes from baseline on a portfolio level, there is also a need for outlier detection in smaller batches or on a per-customer basis. By "Velocity," I mean models looking at out-of-the-ordinary repeat behavior or occurrence of "something." Velocity models come in many shapes and forms—from univariate numerical models looking at purchasing velocity from consumers to clustering algorithms.

Some Velocity Terminology

Univariate velocity models are models counting an individual quantity, such as number of purchases, and responding to changes in that quantity. They are the simplest and most common, because they capture a large number of suspicious activities, either by individual customers or by a group.

A baseline is the normal level of a phenomenon as observed in your data. A baseline is hard to determine in limited data sets, since no history exists to determine standard levels of any type of activity. However, once you have a few million events, you can start to determine what's comon and uncommon for your customers: IPs, email domains, purchase patterns, and more.

Clustering systems, or algorithms, detect groups of cases that have similar values for a number of features or indicators. While univariate models require that you set a threshold or a baseline to compare to and therefore indicate what's okay and what isn't, clustering algorithms are unsupervised. This means that they don't require past examples of good and bad. You get groups of cases, and it's up to you to decide whether to investigate and act on them or not. Of course, with time, you can label certain clusters as belonging to a certain behavior. Clustering algorithms are both slower and significantly more complex than any other model discussed here and, therefore, only used by teams with vast data sets and advanced tools.

Baselining

Spikes in velocity should always be compared to a baseline, and that baseline should be selected wisely. Repeat purchasing behavior for a 65-year-old customer shopping for gardening equipment isn't the same as a 21-year-old college students shopping for clothes. It works the same way with merchants—separating seasonal sales segments from year-round ones will reduce false positives.

Iterative Analysis

Constant analysis of results and definition of velocity root causes—seeing why something popped on your screen and whether it's a previously obesrved behavior—is a key activity to make the best of your velocity tool. Giving names to velocity patterns is exactly like defining any other customer behavior. With time, you'll discover which peaks are clearly good or bad and which require additional attention. Coming back to the previous example, once you detect seasonality, you need to adjust your model to deal with and flag seasonality, and sometimes disregard it while searching for new and unexplained phenomena. Most seasonality is business as usual—a phenomenon to be detected but not to alert your team to or require any change in behavior from your operators.

Individual Merchant/Consumer Velocity Models

Individual models compare number and volume of purchases and sales against a chosen baseline (projections for new merchants, population purchasing behavior for consumers, etc.) to flag those that are more active than usual or whose activity drops (the latter is more relevant to merchants; churned consumers are interesting but not for our current purposes). While hyper-growth volumes aren't necessarily an indication of malicious intent, they can easily drive losses even when the customer means well. A merchant growing in sales beyond their operational capacity may go bankrupt or just create a tidal wave of complaints; an overzealous consumer may try to grab products and run—or is simply on a drunk purchasing binge. All need to be examined and sometimes contacted to alleviate the suspicion or ask for guarantees of continued activity.

General Outlier Detection Models

Many of the trends in your system will not rely on individuals and therefore will not be detected through linking or individual velocity models. General velocity tracks the appearance of individual assets (IP, email domain, zip code, etc.) and flags unusual spikes. This means specific IPs or IP ranges appearing beyond their baseline (an attack, or a promotion at a certain school or work place), new and rare domains spiking (a new free email provider used for fake identities), and others. Univariate velocity models capture most of the outlier activity that is not caught by inflow composition tracking, but depending on your system's complexity, clustering systems may be relevant.

CHAPTER 8

Analysis: Understanding What's Going On

The next step after detecting that something is going on is root cause analysis. Understanding the cause quickly and accurately allows you to solve the current issue as well as prepare for any future changes in the user's behavior. As with anything, proper analysis starts with planning and is highly dependent on the architecture of your system and data availability.

Designing for Analysis

It is hard enough to understand what happens in your system as it is; lacking data, overlapping systems, and bad instrumentation just make it so much harder. When approaching system and data architecture, there are several things to remember that will make your work much easier.

Instrumentation and Data Retention

Many analysis attempts fail due to poor instrumentation and data retention. This usually stems from engineers optimizing for performance and storage size in production code and ends with missing data —since maintaining event-based historical data is not anywhere near the top of these engineers' minds. The simplest example is canceled or rejected applications deleted after a very short while or saved in highly redacted form. When you try to model consumer behavior or merchant performance deterioration patterns based on cancellations and rejections in addition to purchases, you fail due to lack of data. The most advanced example is point-in-time analysis. When you build predictive systems, you always need to be able to look at purchases at the point of approval without post-decision information, but most systems overwrite the purchase object as states change rather than keep snapshots or use an event-based approach.

RMP requires either an event-based system keeping track of each change, or periodical snapshots from almost day one for further analysis. Either way, you must design your system with preparation for future instrumentation and as little data loss as possible.

Data Latency and Transformation

While portfolio analysis sometimes resembles and uses Finance and Business Analysis techniques, most RMP analysis done in order to identify and understand trends and their root cause requires data that are rawer and fresher than what most BI teams require. Therefore, an elaborate data warehouse with long and cumbersome ETL, 24+ latency, and low uptime is an insufficient tool. RMP requires a close to real-time database that is almost a copy of production data but provides some additional capabilities (aggregation, point in time, tuning, and indexing for analysis, etc.).

Most analytics teams use a separate database for analysis. That database is, in its ideal form, a repository that is getting data feeds from production systems and additional services and storing them in an optimized structure for analysis—the data warehouse (DWH). The most common data schema optimized for analysis is called the *star* schema. Production databases are optimized for performance and have very different properties, some of which aren't even relational databases. A process of Extracting, Transforming, and Loading (ETL) the data into the data warehouse is required to make one into the other. Since it's a resource-heavy process requiring and lot of database access, it is usually run in bulk when the service is at lower demand, usually once a day. That is why most data warehouses are up to 24 hours behind compared production databases.

It is often preferable to train your team to use a replicated version of your production database rather than build a highly processed data warehouse. Accordingly, transformation should be basic and bare-bones, as well as thoroughly documented. The time they spend in learning these tools will be saved by more than ten-fold by not having to build elaborate ETL processes and maintain a unique infrastructure for a DWH.

Control Groups

Special attention should be given to instrumentation and control groups that enable decision funnel analytics. Often, your decision funnel consists of several systems working linearly (sometimes even in parallel) to make decisions on applications: rules, models, manual review, etc. Control groups must be implemented across all of your detection systems so you can constantly test your decisions and identify gaps. These control groups should persist through the whole lifecycle—otherwise, the model's control group could be rejected by rules and vice versa. Make sure you design instrumentation and control groups so you can attribute a decision to a specific mechanism and optimize their performance.

Best Practices for Ongoing Analysis

Every system has its idiosyncrasies, and with a large-enough portfolio, most of your analysis will focus on identifying corner cases stemming from interactions between seemingly unrelated product features and operationally driven spikes in costs (mistakes in settlement file parsing are an example). Still, using a few best practices will help you get to a solution earlier and allow you to act faster and with better accuracy.

Automated Segmentation and Tagging

Preserving knowledge from previous investigations is key for iteratively understanding and fixing your loss problems. Having solved a problem once doesn't guaarantee it won't appear again in a few months, by virtue of seasonality or a new big merchant with a clunky operation. Maintain your ability to detect previously solved problems by developing scripts that automatically tag them, and then incrementally add to them as you expand your knowledge. This script suite will serve as the first diagnostic tool you can use on a misbehaving portfolio to single out already known problems and help you focus on the unknowns.

Root Cause Analysis

Once you have a defined subpopulation that needs to be examined further, case-by-case review by domain experts is the next step. The goal is to find the reason behind the loss using careful review in light of all events that transpired after an application was approved. This is where you must combine funnel analytics (knowing which mechanism did or would have acted on this purchase), strong review tools, and investigative capabilities. Talk to your customer (although most of these inquiries provide only half-truths), and follow up on disputes. Many times, customer-care contacts will help you identify integration and process errors. Backtrack everything that happened to the application to understand those.

Analyzing trends in order to find actionable insights is a science (mixed with a little bit of art) requiring deep domain expertise in customer behavior and also detailed understanding of specific systems and processes. Support your team with strong documentation and knowledge sharing in easily searchable databases, and you will create a highly effective investigation process that will properly inform the actions you take.

CHAPTER 9

Action: Dealing with Your Findings

Once you know what needs to be done, using the right tools is the next step. There are several ways to make a change: from ops procedures, through decision systems, and all the way to product changes.

Decision and loss-reduction mechanisms vary by their flexibility, time to market, and impact. Flexibility and time to market improve as you move farther in the application lifecycle—further away from real-time decisions—and impact is reduced accordingly. The lack of flexibility in the front end shouldn't be taken for granted, and a new model's time to market can and should be at the 3 month range rather than the 9–18 months that are most common in large organizations. Still, models vs. rules vs. manual decisions have different advantages and disadvantages and should be used accordingly.

Manual Review

Manually reviewing an application is the core activity of every RMP team. Much like you wouldn't hire a developer who can't write code, you wouldn't want a domain expert that cannot make a decision when reviewing an application. Manual review is not only about making accurate decisions, it is also about knowing when the information you have is insufficient, identifying patterns, and developing a taste for what a mistake looks and feels like. Manual review helps you keep track of your system's pulse and is the basis for more detailed root cause analysis, the most important activity in the problem-solving cycle.

Barring the downsides of a manual operation, discussed previously, the manual review team is the one providing you with the most flexibility for enforcing short-term changes to your decisions without any product changes. Your manual review team must be equipped with a strong application review tool as well as effective and flexible rules governing their backlog. The more flexible the rules are, the better your ability is to feed Ops and make a short-term change.

Manual review is triggered and utilized when a trend is identified by your detection mechanisms. Usually, those come from customer disputes or your linking/velocity mechanisms identifying an activity that you wish to investigate or stop. You need the ability to change your backlog-controlling rules (often referred to as *backend rules* because they run after the purchase has completed and a real-time decision was made) and feed those cases to your review staff so that they can manually stop applications. The process is as ineffective and limited in scope as it is flexible, but it serves as a first response.

Your should also provide review staff with force multipliers, allowing them to make batch decisions on applications as well as translate their insights into broadly applicable actions and rules in your systems. The first step after identifying a new behavior is sending it to review via backend rules. Once a pattern and a response to it have been established, the team should write a rule or a set of rules to automatically handle the new trend. With time, after they get to know this trend and develop a more subtle understanding of how to detect it (best measured by hit rate: every early attempt has low hit rate, but improves over time), detection of this trend can move to real time, and to the model. One of the key obstacles in this process is variables, or indicators, used as building blocks in the rules they write. This is where the Variable Library plays a central role.

The Variable Library

There is a constant gap between the ability to identify, build, and utilize new indicators and data sources in the analysis environment or Ops' sandbox vs. real-time decision mechanisms. Variables get developed separately in two or even three enviornments, by different teams and with different tools, creating a barrier that prevents knowledge from trickling in either direction.

Teaching review staff to look at applications without presenting them with the indicators you use in other systems limits their effectiveness, since inferring why a specific application is rejected, approved, or queued becomes close to impossible. The same happens the other way around: Ops discover a new indicator that can greatly improve decisions and are able to build it in their own silo. Making that indicator/variable available to all services will benefit all decision mechanisms, but without a central variable repository, code gets duplicated and often incorporates bugs. In order to get the positive, compounded effect from models making broad real-time decisions—then rules adding trend detection, then review staff making specific high-impact decisions on new behaviors—you need to provide all with the same data and indicators. Otherwise, you may see different teams solving the same problems using their own tools.

The variable library, or variable service, works to mitigate that. While not a detection or decision mechanism, it is a crucial part of the infrastructure that underlies them. It is a directory of computed variables that makes the same set of variables available to all of your tools: models, rules, manual review, and analysis. Starting early and making this service easy to access and extend solves a major issue in detection improvements as well as many of the bugs inherent to complex model deployment processes. A service-oriented architecture that allows engineers to add new variables on a weekly basis will let you expose front-end variables to your back-end decisions, helping staff make better decisions, as well as allowing Ops to add new variables they they discover while manually reviewing cases and quickly constructing new rules to respond to evolving trends. Those will also trickle into the models in a quicker and smoother fashion.

The Review GUI

A lot of thought is given to data processing and decisions made by agents, but not a lot is given to the tools used to reach those decision and how they support or complicate the investigation process. I discussed this in a 2010 article:

> A lot of times it creeps up on you: volume picks up and so you know you need someone to look at orders. If you're running a small shop it's most probably going to be you, but a lot of companies just hire one or two folks. These people use whatever tool you have to look at transactions—most times a customer service tool—and make up their technique as they go. With time, and sometimes with charge-backs coming in, you realize that your few analysts can't review all transactions, so you turn to set up a few rules to make queue and transaction hold decisions. Since your analysts are not technology people you resort to hard coding some logic based on a product

manager's refinement of the analysts' thoughts, again based on a few (or many) cases they've already seen. Not a long while passes, and you realize that the analysts are caught in a cat and mouse game where they try to create a rule to stop the latest attack that found its way to the chargeback report, and put a lot of strain on the engineers who maintain the rule-set. Even after coding some simple rule writing interface the situation isn't better since the abundance of rules creates unpredictable results, especially if you allowed the rules to actually make automated decisions and place restrictions on transactions and accounts.

Staff is expected to review applications at an ever-growing pace on a collection of interfaces not optimized for their use, either home-grown or based on customer-care systems. There is little variety in off-the-shelf solutions, and the commitment required to build an effective tool (integrating queue management, flow management, a review console pulling all data sources into one place, an so on) is hard to maintain after the first version; the MVP covers 60%—70% of required functionality, and added improvements get constantly down-prioritized against those with higher impact. Manual review and decisions are absolutely required for quality RMP practices, and present-day statistics tell us that manual review is still significantly common. As most Ops staff use at least two systems for review and make decisions, it's obvious that the Ops team needs a strong tool to allow them to do so. This will require at least one engineer constantly tweaking and improving your tools; designing a proper dashboard and review interface that follow agent workflows while enforcing subtle changes for efficiency is essential.

Main Consideration in GUI Design

There are a few key matters to remember when designing or integrating a review interface. Achieving high efficiency and accuracy in review requires human-centric design, compensating for the human factor's shortcomings. People tire, suffer from decision bias and fatigue, and have a hard time assimilating data and using slow systems. A well-designed GUI takes all that into consideration and provides a work environent that's mostly constrained by case quality rather than inadequate tools; it can support your team and give them the best possible environment for high performance.

Decision Fatigue

Making a decision every few minutes for hours on end is tiring, even with planned breaks. Analysis of previous mistakes and detailed KPIs, while driving better performance, contribute to fear of mistakes and decision bias. All of these together cause *decision fatigue*, usually reflected in agents deferring to others by starting group discussions about cases, calling the customer, and so on. Your review tool must support flow management that escalates these cases to an experienced staffer that will make a quicker, more efficient decision; this way, you let your team defer a decision (which is sometimes unavoidable and needed) but still get the case worked quickly. Layering expertise and difficulty levels allows new employees to deal with the bulk of the work you're trying to simplify and automate, while your senior employees make high-impact decisions.

System Responsiveness

Review staff spend a lot of their time waiting for pages to load. While your page load times and system responsiveness don't need to be at consumer product levels, the number of clicks to decision and wait time between pages need to be reasonable. Three to five clicks per decision and up to ten seconds of wait are not ideal, but allow page switching without excessive memorization—one of the leading reasons for wrong decisions. The best option is a single page.

Data Assimilation

Review staff also suffer from context switching. There is only so much copying and pasting you can do between your main screen and whitepages or social network sites that you may be using for your review without making errors, and comparing details becomes a tedious job. Make sure that your interface prepopulates as much information as possible from external sources on a single page and that those data are organized in a way that complements your review method. Use color coding and imagery to highlight important details or ones that require more investigation.

The Rules Engine

The rules engine is practically where "it" all should happen. In basic or early implementations of RMP systems, "rule" refered to a piece of hard-coded logic describing a specific behavior or trigger. (More than three purchases today? IP country doesn't match billing address?) and queueing applications for review (or rejecting them upfront). A proper rules engine, however, is an interface (whether graphical or not) that allows non-developers to draw data from various sources (external, complete models, or your variable service) and compose statements in a syntax that allows sophisticated arguments—regular expressions, string manipulation, and some flow control commands such as IF statements and FOR loops.

Basic Functionality Requirements

The rules engine should have at least decision tree functionality—allowing you to segment an incoming population and set different reject and queue thresholds for different groups of applications—as well as the ability to quickly write and deploy simple rules that will respond to an evolving trend. While functionality should be the same across the application lifecycle, the rules engine should be able to connect and provide different permission levels and controls for real-time and async rule sets, as both are important but mistakes will be significantly costlier in the frontend.

Performance Simulation

In order to effectively deliver quick value through changes in rule-based decisions, you need to see a what-if simulation—showing the performance of that rule on its own as well as its incremental benefit to the overall rule set. You need to measure rule performance, identify ones that will not contribute to your optimization goal, and retire those that are not helpful anymore. Poor rule-set management results in code spaghetti (this is especially true for hard-coded rules that cannot be easily changed). Extensive performance simulation before you let a rule impact your application flow prevents suboptimization. It is possible for new rules to target a bad population that is only slightly incremental to the current rule set, but introduce a large set of false positives, thus reducing overall performance. Simulation and validation (checking for syntax errors and possibly logic errors) are vital, especially for short lived rules.

Performance Monitoring

Funnel analytics should be mentioned once again. Being able to measure rules as a set and individually for performance tweaking and retirement is a key component in managing your decision funnel. Implementing and instrumenting the rules engine's actions must be planned in advance, as well as the data infrastructure supporting both its real-time actions and reporting needs.

Automated Decision Models

For simplification purposes, the word *modeling* is used in this book to describe the construction of any type of automatic decision. Regression, classification, clustering, and other techniques aren't discussed separately. For all purposes, modeling is a process that consumes a set of indicators, or "features," and turns them into a score for a given action. The score tells you how "bad" the purchase is (the definition of bad can change), or how much it fits a specific profile you're trying to detect. A threshold score is then determined for each score range; any action getting a score equal to or higher than the threshold will be let through, and those below it will be stopped or reviewed manually. As the threshold becomes lower, you can expect more approved actions and more losses. Finding the optimal threshold for your business is therefore an important decision.

Building a model is a complicated, detail-oriented task. You will start by using statistical models roughly 6–12 months into your company's life, depending on growth trajectory, and they will become a very important tool in your decision-making process, as they are the best for making automated decisions at scale. Using models depends not only on the number and total amount of purchases that go through your system, but also the diversity of your population and the number of bad purchases you see. If you acquire one type of customer through one channel and sell one type of product (say you have a t-shirt printing businesses selling wholesale to small brick-and-mortar businesses at festivals), you'll need a smaller sample. As complexity grows, so do the requirements of your data. I'd like to touch upon several pitfalls and issues to remember when building models for RMP.

What Are You Predicting?

Training set construction and feature engineering are much more effective when the predicted class or performance flag are clearly defined. A class or performance flag are two ways of naming what it is that the model is trying to predict. Depending on the type of problem and type of algorithm, you could try to predict anything from the probability of default on a certain purchase to whether an individual IP belongs to a government agency. I use several classes, corresponding to the main archetypes of behavior (fraud, default, abuse, and technical errors), that are predicted separately and then combined into a single decision flow. With a small sample, splitting by different classes will almost guarantee model over-fitting. When choosing a single flag (usually loss/not loss), other problems arise: although you may make the same decision for two very similar purchases, they could randomly get very different treatment from the Collections team, an effect that is almost impossible to separate. Starting from a flag indicating, per purchase, whether it has or hasn't caused loss is a first step; then, separately predicting specific behaviors that are easy to identify directly is the way to go from a general performance flag to multiple ones.

Which Algorithms Should You Use?

With the rise in popularity of data science, there sometimes seems to be pressure to use sophisticated techniques and algorithms regardless of their actuall business impact. The fact is that, more often than not, the simplest tools are the ones with the best impact as well as the most easily interpreted results. Some highly touted algorithms are more accurate but require much more computing power, hence limiting scale or the amount of data you can use in real time; some are black boxes and thus harder to tune and improve, especially for smaller data sets. Layering regression models that target different behaviors and proper feature engineering that captures interaction will create a much stronger prediction system. Especially in RMP, a practice assuming the existence of an adversary, being able to interpret loss events, and tune your system is critical. You must be able to tie a loss event to a root cause through all decisions taken on an application in your system.

Model Time to Market (TTM)

TTM measures the time it takes to launch a model from initial analysis to 100% live performance. Short time to market matters because it means you quickly respond to changes in your customer population. However, most RMP teams aren't properly set up for short TTM. Usually, the analytics team is separate from the engineering team and is providing the latter with specs for developed models in a waterfall development model. As a result, models go through several reimplementation and compilation processes (first at analytics, then in engineering), causing bugs and delays, demonstrating the lack of shared language and tools between analysts and engineers. It is not uncommon for new models to go through a few months of tuning while the analytics team detects bugs and the engineering team fixes them. The Variable Service mentioned earlier is one possible solution to the problem, since it serves the same variables/features in development and production. The Rules Engine provides the ability to write and deploy segmentation and flow logic easily, thus allowing code reuse instead of reimplementation from scratch with every version. You should build your RMP service to use these components wisely and reduce model TTM significantly.

TTM is so impactful that if you can guarantee TTM shorter than a month you can lax the controls preventing over-fitting. Over-fitting is a situation that may occur for various reasons in which a model predicts a random phenomenon represented in the data instead of an actual relationship. When samples are too small, random events of even small magnitude seem much more important than they are in reality, therefore skewing the model's performance. In plain English, the model "thinks" that this phenomenon is very common and therefore doesn't "give enough attention" to other, more important ones, thus not learning how to predict them effectively. As time passes, even very well built models' performance degrades and decisions become less accurate as behaviors shift. That degradation slows down significantly when you start to identify archetypes of customer behaviors that don't significantly change, but until then, performance degradation can be so steep that shorter model deployment cycles provide much greater value than elaborate and complex feature engineering and model tuning. Since your data sets are small, you're guaranteed to constantly find new behaviors that just didn't appear a month or two ago, and the model did not train on. If your model refreshes every month, it may over-represent behaviors that were observed in the previous month, but since those constantly change, that's not a big problem. Of course, once you reach a standard set of features and behaviors you're targeting, or a large enough data set, this stops being true. For many teams that I've seen, though, a standard set of features and behaviors is a stretch goal even after years of operation.

The Feedback Loop

You will get feedback from losses, but false positives and some false negatives will systematically not be detected. Most of your rejected customers will not try again, leaving you to think that they were rightfully rejected, and surprisingly, not all customers impacted by fraud will complain. As discussed previously regarding domain experts and manual feedback, you must sample applications and have domain experts manually review them. Without this crucial step, you will always be limited to effects that have significant representation in your existing data set, since these are the only ones the model will learn from. As a result, expanding your customer base will be difficult and require large-scale controlled experiments where you allow previously rejected customers through. An automated system cannot make "leaps of faith" or infer correctly whether a very small sample of a newly detected behavior is good or bad. As a result, if your system is automated and you want to expand into a new industry segment, a country, or maybe reject fewer applications, your best option is to randomly approve previously rejected applications and wait for losses to come in so you can learn from them. While this is possible, it is a slow process that usually requires high "tuition" costs, paid for in losses. Domain-expert-based control will allow you to reach conclusions faster and often more accurately, as they are expected to correctly generalized on small samples and come up with features that will allow accurate detection.

Product and Experience Modifications

RMP teams focus on real-time and post-approval detection and prevention of risk and loss. Loss can also be managed and reduced by changes to customer experience. Specific experiences can be used to handle heterogeneous groups of applications that contain both customers you'd like to reject as well as ones you'd like to approve, but are too indistinguishable with the information given to you regularly by all customers. That's when you throw a question or additional step at them and judge by their response.

In-Flow Challenges

In-flow challenges are a "nicer" way for getting customers to go through a few extra hoops before getting approved. These sometimes are designed to respond to a specific attack vector, asking the fraudster to do something that most probably only the real person can do. Another option is challenges that put the customer in a specific mindset before applying for a loan or making a purchase, making them more aware of the commitment they are making.

An example of the former is KBA, knowledge-based authentication, used when signing up to package-tracking services online. Identity theft is common in the US, and consumers' identities can be used to re-route packages to fraudster drop points or re-shippers, who are often innocent people working from home, unaware that they are aiding an act of fraud. KBA will ask you a few questions, based on your credit report, that the average person will not be able to answer without extensive research: a past spouse, historical addresses, and so on. While definitely not fool or fraud proof, this reduces the chances of simple identity fraud.

An example of the latter is an alert prompting the consumer to rethink an action before submitting it. While considered a conversion-killing crime, when very specifically targeted it can pinpoint problematic customers. Several online retailers started using this kind of alert for impulse buyers who use their websites while drunk on weekends. Though a lot of them paid, this proved to be a highly remorseful crowd who often returned items, and some retailers chose to discourage them than have to deal with restocking and chargebacks.

User Experience Changes

A lot of losses can be prevented in advance by creating a more accommodating user experience that takes specific customer needs into consideration. This is an especially effective way of dealing with merchant-driven losses. Merchant risk management is different than most consumer risk effort since it's a long-term process that deals with different risks. Insolvency and operational issues are common. As a result, merchant risk requires a lot of interaction with and information from the merchant. Most of these operations still use printed, faxed, and scanned documents and are unsuccessful in getting merchants to cooperate freely and provide timely information. What they end up doing is placing limitations on merchants with even the smallest deviations from a generally acceptable baseline.

The most common risk-prevention mechanism for commercial credit is a reserve—holding a certain amount, often a few days' worth of payments or a certain percentage of turnover, as hedge against possible losses. Reserves are used by both offline and online services providers. Merchants are not fond of reserves; cash flow is severely impacted by them, and at least in some cases reserves lead to small-merchant insolvency. A more sophisticated alternative is merchant lifecycle management, prompting merchants to provide you more information at strategic points—after the first purchase, before the first payout, when they start experiencing hyper-growth—when they are motivated to cooperate in order to get their business going. That way, instead of slapping a one-size-fits-all reserve that never changes and puts a strain on all merchants at all times, you can respond to higher risk levels when warranted. Smart user experience design is required to provide this kind of smooth lifecycle management experience. When properly done, it is much more effective than reserves and creates good will with merchants as you help them grow their business.

Proactive Risk Management

The last option I mentioned is proactively promoting customer safety by making them change a password or add more defense mechanisms (such as additional secret codes). This should happen when you discover a real or potential breach in your system or a related service—the equivalent of a security patch in software. The evolution of credit card seurity codes demonstrates this: when stolen credit cards started to include the front of the card from in-store charge slips, the issuers added a three-digit number to the back of the card. When that started to be collected by fraudsters, they added another secret—a code on your statement, 3D-secure.

Some websites proactively trigger mass password resets when they discover a breach. This happens every once in a while. In January 2013, Twitter did exactly that. Roughly 250,000 account passwords were reset, possibly due to a third-party app being hacked. This tactic has proven useful multiple times.

When Things Go Wrong: Dispute Resolution

Many RMP teams focus on detection and prevention as closely as possible to real time. That's a reasonable effort. The closer to in-flow you make a correct decision, the better return on invested time. Dealing with losses after they occur costs more time and money than stopping them from happening. That focus, however, sometimes obscures the fact that (a) losses happen anyway and (b) there is much to be recovered by proper handling of disputes when they happen. I've touched on this subject earlier in this book: a large chunk of losses are actually a misunderstanding. When properly handled, some of those could be prevented from turning into chargebacks, and even if they do, can be disputed and won. There are two major things to think about when designing and operating a dispute process for small and medium companies: experience design and back-office efficiency.

User Experience Design

UX in dispute resolutions encompasses all the emails, text messages, web pages, and phone call scripts a customer interacts with. These have a profound impact on whether you'll be able to reduce losses as well as provide the customer with a brand-supporting experience that will result in them coming back. Your first and foremost goal is to establish credibility with the customer and have them settle their dispute through you rather than through a third party and to feel that they've been treated fairly, even if you have decided against them. Working with third parties (an issuing bank or a mediator) is a cumbersome and painful process for both them and you. If you establish credibility by allowing customers to submit a dispute and handling it fairly—by communicating early and often and sharing progress whenever possible—you will be able to handle most disputes in-house and, if nothing else, reduce process-related fees that you'd incur from dealing with external parties.

The second design goal is reminding customers that they are actually good customers and that a fair settlement is in the best interest for all parties involved. It is never fun to be the victim of identity fraud, but a good number of "fraud" victims actually gave explicit or implied permission to a family member (child or spouse) to use their card or made a risky business decision that backfired. When reminded, or confronted with purchasing and usage behavior in a consumer's case, most of them find that this was the case. Some consumers try to dodge payments through denial of purchases they obviously made; denial of future service causes many of them to square up to not be cut off. Finally, quite a lot of customers do want to pay but run into temporary financial problems. Giving them the ability to negotiate the timing and amounts they will pay to settle their debt will allow more of them to pay you in full.

Back Office Efficiency

Dispute resolution is a manual process, plagued with low impact when handled incorrectly. As a result, many companies do not spend energy on it. Businesses with tight margins must care about dispute resolution and specifically about making it streamlined. Chargeback challenge, proving to the bank that a certain chargeback has no merit, is a process that you must at least consider. Like any other operational process, you must pay attention to detail; responses must match the chargeback code you received and include correct evidence. If you follow the strict (and sometimes confusing) guidelines, you'll improve you ability to recoup losses. Some analysis of the process and simple automation will boost your recovery significantly. While chargeback management is a highly manual and detail-oriented business, the potential for higher recovery on your losses is a direct contribution to your bottom line.

Setting Up Your Team and Tools

Now that you have a good sense of what you're trying to solve, how do you measure and detect phenomena and performance and determine how to improve them? How do you start getting it done? Should you build everything yourself? What's already out there, and how much is it going to cost you? How do you make a buy vs. build decision, and if you don't build, how do you make sure you're not completely dependent on your providers?

Buy vs. Build

Buy vs. build depends on what is or isn't core competence for your company, the stage you're at, and the availability of data and resources.

The need for core competence is different for retailers vs. other participants in the payments ecosystem and is tied to business model and margins. If you act as a non-risk-taking agent for financial services providers or have zero cost of goods sold (like most virtual goods and gaming companies), you will be less sensitive to losses and have a higher margin to pay for tools and products. Lifecycle stage is another consideration: companies in hypergrowth should generally pay a third party and invest engineering and hustling efforts in whatever contributes directly to the top line. On the other hand, if your margins are tight, you're operating a mature business, or risk is a core feature of your product (short-term lending falls in this category), you'll want to keep at least some of the activity and capabilities in-house.

The availability of engineering resources is an obvious constraint, as you'll want to invest effort in the work that will contribute most to your growth. That is, as discussed previously, the main reason for the destructive cycle causing RMP product work to be constantly underfunded: the need to invest ahead of time is unclear, major loss events are the main driver to action, and time constraints force patchy solutions. When this starts hitting you, buying a third-party solution makes more sense. Data availability is slightly different: if you have large historical datasets and/or access to data no one else has (e.g., you're working for Facebook, LinkedIn, PayPal, Amazon, etc.), you are better positioned to develop proprietary in-house RMP tools. Others who are bootstrapping their database or are in need of standardized data (e.g., credit scores) will pay a lot of money to attain access to those.

Which Vendors Should You Look For?

No matter your engineering team size or data availability, there is always something you'll need to buy. What's available, and where should you look? The following is in no way an exhaustive or up-to-date list, but rather a few points to think of when you start shopping.

Should You Buy an Off-the-Shelf Risk System?

Unless you're a huge and profitable payments company or retailer that needs a simplified, interactive tool for legions of operators with little technical training, stay away from using detection platforms with fancy GUIs and built-in detection models. Outsourcing your risk decisions isn't necessarily a bad idea, as discussed before, but these systems specifically have multiple downsides. First, they are expensive. Integrating a system that costs six to seven figures is far from a good investment for most businesses. Second, such systems seldom integrate at multiple touch points. Integration is limited to front-end detection, missing on additional data from back-end decisions and disputes. Even when this functionality exists, integration time prohibits a full integration. As a result, lack of a full feedback loop for front-end models produces suboptimal decisions. Finally, since these companies do not provide any guarantee, your financial interests are not fully aligned, and you are left dealing with wrong decisions.

If RMP is not core to your business, seek a company that is easy to integrate with, delivers decisions rather than recommendations, and takes your loss liability. That is the best buying ROI decision. The one obvious exception to this "only buy decisions" rule is if you're breaking into a new market or segment and a provider has a lot of historical information that you can temporarily use while entering the market such that the high cost makes sense. For example, credit scores in a new country you're expanding into; there are credit bureaus in many countries that could charge you several dollars per hit but will provide a lot of helpful data and scoring. That makes sense to pay for as you're expanding, and while expensive, is in no way at the same price level as a full suite of tools.

Detection Vendors and Social Data

Some companies sell detection services, identifying specific behaviors that are either hard to detect or require industry data to detect effectively. One of the most common ones is returning-user detection and "device fingerprinting," telling you whether a user visiting your website has already visited with different details or has been flagged as bad on a different website. Others sell blacklists of stolen and compromised accounts and consumer details to validate against. Most of these are pretty expensive, and make sense only if you're price insensitive. Blacklists and device ID can be built in-house with 60%–70% accuracy in a few weeks, and given the integration time and complexity required by most vendors, their main advantage is providing industry-wide monitoring based on their customer base. If you're selling virtual goods and are under constant attack, you're in their sweet spot and will see a lot of benefit even at this price level. If you're selling candy and have kids using their parents' identity, you won't see as much benefit. As usual, understanding your problems is key to solving them.

A few providers in Europe and the US offer identity validation and social network data enrichment—giving you additional information about an individual based on email, and sometimes name and address. Most of them are shipping and marketing companies that found a way to aggregate and resell the data they collect. While you should first make sure you're protecting yourself from privacy policy violations when using these vendors, they provide interesting data allowing you to eliminate fake identities as well as learn more about your customers. The main problem, however, is coverage; different providers have different datasets that are often incomplete and only occasionally overlap, requiring you to integrate with all of them and spend effort on piecing the puzzle together in your database. Instead, use an aggregator of social and identity data that can give you slightly or heavily processed data that you can use in your decision process.

Must-Have Tools and Data Sources

There are tools and data sources I always use, because their ROI is high and justify using them in any case. AVS and other address-to-card validation sources are a no brainer and usually come as an add-on from your payment gateway. IP geolocation and network type are also extremely cheap compared to other data sources and will help you detect proxies, suspicious, and safe connections rather easily. Email provider type, usually provided by the same companies, can help you separate unknown but free email domains and other blacklisted ones. Google Maps' (or other providers') address type and geolocation APIs are a helpful source to see where your package is being sent and suspicious addresses. Some incredibly cheap databases will tell you whether the phone you got from the user is a mobile, VoIP, or fixed line. All of these are good and rather easy to integrate tools that you should look into when you're starting to build internal capabilities, but won't provide final and liability-shifting decisions. Still, most of these sources can be replaced with internal data if your database is large enough.

Don't Forget Domain Expertise

Outsourcing decisions and using external data sources is often a good idea, but does not mean you should stop growing and nurturing internal domain expertise. Your internal team should be much more than an operator of a black-box rule system. Even when outsourcing parts of your process you must have analytics and manual review to track your vendors' performance, manually review selected samples, and examine false positives in multiple segments. The operational and analytical parts of your RMP functions may be smaller, but shouldn't disappear, or you'll be at the mercy of your vendor. Make sure that even if you decide to completely bypass dealing with RMP, you have at least one person that has it as part of their job description to see what kind of value for money you're getting. It will save you a lot.

Epilogue

Risk management for online payments is part science and analytics, part product management, part operations management, part UX design, and part art. It is an interdisciplinary field that is only at the beginning of its growth as a discipline. That growth as well as our ever-resourceful adversaries make this a fascinating field to be involved in, even if sometimes nerve-wracking. In this book, I've tried to piece together an introduction, laying out the major points you need to think about when starting and running an effective RMP team. As always, our goal is to create delightful experiences for our customers; a safe, accurate and courteous RMP team is one that makes sure bad things don't happen on your platform and buys you credibility when they do (and they will). I am hopeful that you found this book helpful and that it will help spark a conversation regarding RMP best practices as well as attract more smart, entrepreneurial individuals to the realm of online security.

San Francisco, Spring 2013.

Further contact, feedback, and questions welcome at *www.ohadsamet.com*.

Have it your way.

Get even more for your money.